Contents

Terms and Techniques

Throughout this book, you will find various knitting terms and techniques that may or may not be familiar to you. Refer to this section if you encounter an unfamiliar term or technique or if you need to refresh your memory on how to knit a particular stitch.

GAUGE

The concept of making a gauge swatch is not popular with many knitters, but if you want your hat or mittens to turn out the way you expect, you must take the time to make a gauge swatch! If I could tell every knitter one thing about gauge, it's this: *you don't have to use the size needle that is called for in the pattern.* Every knitter is different; some are loose knitters (like me), some are tight knitters, and some knit at the same tension as that mysterious person who decided to specify a needle size on the yarn's ball band. Since I'm a loose knitter, I normally start my swatch with a needle that is at least one size smaller. The information on the yarn's ball band can provide helpful information about needle size in addition to what is specified in the pattern. *Remember this: It's not your job to change your knitting style, it's only your job to find the size needle that allows you to knit at the same gauge as the pattern.*

Generally, the gauge is specified for the main body of knitting on the item, and the first needle that is listed in the needle section is the size that is "recommended" to achieve that gauge. For instance on a mitten, the gauge is for the stockinette stitch portion that is made after the ribbing is completed. If you use a needle that is different than the one specified in the pattern, then you will also need to change the needle size used for the ribbing as well. Generally this needle will be two sizes smaller. Once you find the size needle you need in order to achieve the correct gauge, then use a needle for the ribbing that is proportionally smaller. For instance, imagine working with a pattern that calls for a size 7 (4.5 mm) for the gauge swatch and 5 (3.75 mm) for the ribbing. If you find that you need a size 6 (4 mm) to achieve the gauge, then you will need a size 4 (3.5 mm) for the ribbing.

When knitting in the round it's a good idea to swatch in the round because the majority of your work will be in stockinette stitch (all knit), and most knitters work purl stitches at a different tension compared to knit stitches. I normally cast on 30 to 40 stitches and join them in the round for my swatch. I swap needles in and out until I feel I'm getting the correct gauge and *then I knit for a few more inches to be sure.*

SLIPPING STITCHES

Unless otherwise stated, a stitch should be slipped as if to purl which maintains its orientation relative to the needle.

SLIPPING KNITWISE AND PURLWISE

Slipping a stitch simply means moving it from the left needle to the right needle without knitting or purling it. A stitch is slipped knitwise by inserting the right needle from the front to the back (as if you were getting ready to knit) and then moving it to the right needle. A stitch is slipped purlwise by inserting the right needle from the back to the front (as if you were getting ready to purl) and then moving it to the right needle.

WITH YARN IN FRONT (WYIF)
WITH YARN IN BACK (WYIB)

These are terms often associated with slip stitch patterns and they simply refer to where the working yarn is when the stitch is slipped, either in front of the needle (wyif) or behind the needle (wyib).

INCREASES

LIFTED INCREASE (INC)

Tilt your work slightly so you can see the back side of the knitting. Use your right needle to lift up the loop from the stitch that's directly below the stitch on your left needle (1). Place this loop on your left needle (2) and knit into it (3) thereby adding an extra stitch.

KNIT FRONT AND BACK (KF&B)

This is known as the bar increase because a small bar is formed on the right side of the knitting.

First knit in the usual way but don't take the new stitch off your left needle (4). Pivot the right needle to the back of the left needle and insert it knitwise (from front to back) into the back loop of the same stitch just worked. Make another stitch into the back loop (5). Slip the old stitch off the left needle. There are now two stitches in place of one.

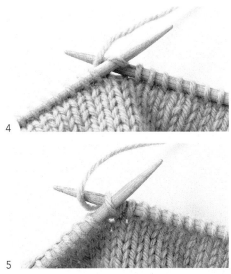

PURL FRONT AND BACK (PF&B)

First purl in the usual way but don't take the new stitch off the left needle. Keeping the working yarn in front, pivot the right needle to the back of the left needle and insert it purlwise (from back to front) into the back loop of the same stitch just worked (6). Make another purl stitch in the back loop. Slip the old stitch off the left needle. There are now two stitches in place of one.

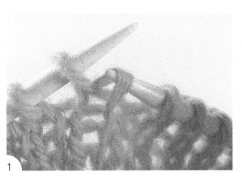

MAKE ONE (M1)

Several different versions of the make one increase are used in this book and they all have in common the fact that they make a stitch out of the horizontal bar or "ladder" that extends between every two stitches. The bar is picked up onto the left needle and then worked as a knit stitch or a purl stitch. The increase is caused to slant by how the bar is picked up, either from the front or the back. This type of increase leaves a tiny hole at the base of the new stitch.

MAKE ONE LEFT (M1L)

Working from front to back, insert left needle under the horizontal bar between the stitch on the right needle and the stitch on the left needle (1). Knit this strand through the back loop to give it a twist (2).

MAKE ONE LEFT PURL (M1LP)

To work the same increase on the purl side, insert the left needle from front to back under the horizontal bar and work a purl stitch through the back loop.

MAKE ONE RIGHT (M1R)

Working from back to front insert left needle under the horizontal bar between the stitch on the right needle and the stitch on the left needle. Knit this strand through the front loop to give it a twist.

MAKE ONE RIGHT PURL (M1RP)

To work the same increase on the purl side insert the left needle from back to front under the horizontal bar and work a purl stitch through the front loop.

YARNOVER (YO)

Bring yarn forward between needles and lay it over the right needle in a counter clockwise direction ending behind the needle. Knit the next stitch (3). Notice that the yarnover has made an extra loop on the right needle that will be worked as a stitch on the next row.

BACKWARD THUMB LOOP

This is essentially a cast-on that adds one or more stitches at the beginning of a row or to be used for shaping. Wrap the working yarn around left thumb from front to back and use your other fingers to hold the yarn end firmly against your palm (4). Insert the right needle upward into the loop, release it from your left thumb, and transfer the loop to the right needle (5).

PURL THREE TOGETHER (P3TOG)

Work as for p2tog but insert right needle into next three stitches on left needle.

SLIP, SLIP, KNIT (SSK)

This decrease is very similar to the k2tog except that the decrease is worked through the back loops of two stitches at a time. Working one at a time, slip two stitches knitwise to right needle (8). Insert the tip of the left needle into the front loops of these two stitches. Knit these stitches at the same time through the back loops as if they were one stitch (9).

DECREASES

KNIT TWO TOGETHER (K2TOG)

Insert the right needle knitwise into the next two stitches on the left needle. Knit these two stitches at the same time as if they were one stitch (6).

KNIT THREE TOGETHER (K3TOG)

Work as for k2tog but insert right needle into next three stitches on left needle.

PURL TWO TOGETHER (P2TOG)

Insert the right needle purlwise into the next two stitches on the left needle. Purl these two stitches at the same time as if they were one stitch (7).

PASS SLIP STITCH OVER (PSSO)

Slip the first stitch on the left needle knitwise, then knit the next stitch on the left needle. Use the left needle tip to pick up the slipped stitch and pass it over the knit stitch just made and off the end of the right needle.

CABLES AND TWIST STITCHES

FOUR-STITCH RIGHT KNIT CROSS (4-ST RKC)

Slip next 2 stitches purlwise to cable needle and hold at back of work (1), knit next 2 stitches from left needle, knit 2 stitches from cable needle (2).

SIX-STITCH RIGHT KNIT CROSS (6-ST RKC)

Slip next 3 stitches purlwise to cable needle and hold at back of work, knit next 3 stitches from left needle, knit 3 stitches from cable needle.

TWO-STITCH RIGHT TWIST (2-ST RT)

K2tog but don't take the stitches off the left needle, there will be one new stitch on the right needle (3). Insert right needle into first stitch on left needle (4), knit it and then remove both stitches from left needle. Two new stitches have been formed on the right needle and the stitch count remains the same.

1

2

3

4

OTHER TECHNIQUES

PICK UP AND KNIT

Stitches are added to an already knitted edge by picking up and knitting. This is a confusing term; you aren't actually *knitting* the stitch as you pick it up. Rather, the stitch is picked up *knitwise* onto the right needle to be knit on the next round or row. Working from the right side, insert the right needle from front to back going under two strands* along the edge (5). Wrap the yarn around the needle as if you were knitting and pull a loop through and onto the right needle (6). Continue in this manner until the required stitches have been added. *On occasion when picking up stitches for mittens, only one strand will be available.*

5

6

WORKING IN THE ROUND— STOCKINETTE STITCH AND GARTER STITCH

Working in the round differs from knitting back and forth. To work stockinette stitch in the round, every round is knit. To work garter stitch in the round, a purl round is alternated with a knit round. For more information about knitting these two stitches in the round see Hat Extras, page 24.

READING PATTERNS

You will find two special symbols in patterns, * * and [ ]. Both are used to indicate a repeat in the round. Generally directions between asterisks such as *k2, p2* are repeated over and over to the end of the round or until a specified number of stitches remain. Likewise, directions between brackets are repeated a number of times before proceeding to another set of directions on that round. For instance, [k2, p2] twice means that you will k2, p2, k2, p2 before working the next set of directions in the round.

MULTIPLE SIZES

Because most of the patterns are written for a range of sizes, it will be necessary to determine which directions apply to the size you are making. In most cases, a chart will be shown which defines the dimensions of a particular size and for the sake of simplicity gives that size a name; Size 1, Size 2, Size 3, etc. Following the chart you will find the specification of how the directions for the sizes will be shown in the pattern using one or more sets of parentheses. For example, the Mitten Power 5.0, page 18 is written in eight sizes. The directions are shown in this order: Size 1 (Size 2, Size 3, Size 4, Size 5, Size 6, Size 7, Size8). The first line of the pattern reads: *Cast on 28 (32, 33, 36) (36, 40, 40, 44) sts.* If you're making size 3, which is the middle direction inside the first parentheses, then you will cast on 32 stitches.

When working from a pattern with a large number of sizes, it's a good idea to photocopy the pattern before you start so you can highlight all the directions applying to the size you are making. In defense of hard-working authors and designers, I must implore you to only make copies from a book for your own use and not share with others.

You will notice that the some of the rows have a lot of information in terms of which size the directions apply to. Please pay careful attention (this is where highlighting is so helpful). If the row doesn't specify a particular size then you can assume that it applies to all sizes.

Mitten Basics

Mittens may seem a bit daunting to make because of their shape, but once you follow the step-by-step directions you'll be amazed by how simple it is to make a pair. The most complicated part is casting on to double-pointed needles but after that it's smooth sailing. These basic mittens are knit out of worsted weight wool.

STEP-BY-STEP- GUIDE FOR KNITTING MITTENS

This step-by-step guide is intended for the knitter who has never made a pair of mittens. Knitting directions are written in plain text, followed by further explanation in italics.

Human hands have much more variation in size than heads so you'll find many sizes to choose from. When working from a pattern with a large number of sizes, it's a good idea to photocopy the pattern before you start so you can highlight all the directions applying to the size you are making.

GAUGE

20 sts = 4" (10 cm) in stockinette stitch

Important: Make a gauge swatch before you start knitting. It's the only way to make sure the mittens will turn out the way you expect (see page 2).

YARN

Medium weight yarn; approximate yardage for each size is shown in chart.

Shown: Cascade Yarns *220 Wool*, 100% wool; 220 yd (201 m) per 3.5 oz (100 g) skein

NEEDLES AND NOTIONS

US size 7 (4.5 mm) double-pointed needles or size required to achieve gauge

US size 5 (3.75 mm) double-pointed needles (or two sizes smaller than size used to achieve gauge)

Circular stitch markers

Small stitch holder (or waste yarn)

Yarn needle for weaving in ends

MITTEN BASICS: Size, Finished Dimensions, and Yardage

	To Fit Size	Finished Hand Circumference	Finished Length	Approximate Yardage
Size 1	2 to 4 year	5½" (14 cm)	5¾" (15 cm)	60 yd (55 m)
Size 2	5 to 7 year	6¼" (16 cm)	7" (18 cm)	80 yd (73 m)
Size 3	8 to 10 year	6¾" (17 cm)	7¾" (20 cm)	100 yd (91 m)
Size 4	12 year to Women's Small	7¼" (18 cm)	8½" (22 cm)	110 yd (101 m)
Size 5	Women's Medium	7½" (19 cm)	9" (23 cm)	130 yd (119 m)
Size 6	Women's Large/Men's Small	8" (20 cm)	9¾" (25 cm)	150 yd (137 m)
Size 7	Men's Medium	8½" (22 cm)	10½" (27 cm)	175 yd (160 m)
Size 8	Men's Large	9" (23 cm)	11½" (29 cm)	195 yd (173 m)

Directions will be shown in the pattern as follows: Size 1 (Size 2, Size 3, Size 4) (Size 5, Size 6, Size 7, Size 8)

CAST ON STITCHES
AND BEGIN KNITTING CUFF

Make both mittens alike.

Using smaller needles, cast on 28 (32, 32, 36) (36, 40, 40, 44) sts. Place BOR marker and join in the round being careful not to twist.

Double-pointed needles generally come in sets of five. The stitches can be divided between three or four needles; the extra free needle is used to knit. If you are using three needles then a triangle will be formed; four needles form a square. Cast on all the required stitches for the size you are making to one needle and then transfer them, evenly divided, to the other two or three needles (1).

2

3

1

It is important that the stitches not be twisted when joining to knit mittens in the round. Lay the needles down on a table in a triangle (2) or square (3) making sure that the bump at the bottom of the stitches is lined up facing the center of the triangle (or square). The first stitch that was cast on is on the left needle and the last stitch, connected to the working yarn, is on the right needle.

Keeping the needles in this arrangement, pick them up and use the free needle to begin knitting into the first cast-on stitch on the left needle using the working yarn from the last stitch on the right needle (4). Knit all of the stitches from the left needle on to the free needle. When the left needle is empty it becomes the new free needle and is used to knit the stitches on the next needle and so on. Note that you will begin the k2, p2 pattern on the very first row.

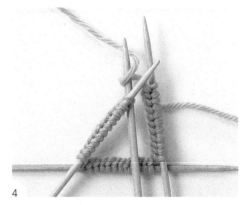

4

Round 1: *K2, p2*; repeat from * to * to end of round.

Repeat round 1 until cuff measures 1½" (2", 2¼", 2½") (2½", 2¾", 2¾", 3") [4 (5, 6, 6.5) (6.5, 7, 7, 7.5) cm].

The best way to deal with the extra needles holding stitches waiting to be worked is to ignore them! Focus on the two needles being used at any given time and hold them to the front while the other needles stay out of the way to the sides and back (5). If you find that the needles are falling out of the stitches while you work then change to longer double-pointed needles or bamboo needles if you are using metal ones.

Once you have knit an entire round place a marker to indicate the beginning of the round. You may find it easier to keep the BOR marker in its place if you readjust the stitches so that the marker falls in the middle of a needle.

THUMB GUSSET

In preparation to make the thumb gusset some adjustments will be made to the stitch count. Also note that you will be changing to the larger needles since the ribbing section is now finished.

Change to larger needles.

Round 1: Knit.

Round 2 for sizes 1, 2, 3, and 4: Inc 1, knit to end of round.

Round 2 for sizes 5, 6, 7, and 8: Knit.

Round 3 for sizes 5, 6, 7, and 8 only: Inc 1, knit to end of round. Skip for other sizes.

There should be:
29 (33, 33, 37) (37, 41, 41, 45) sts.

The thumb gusset is a triangular-shaped addition that is formed by increasing stitches on one side of the mitten. The increases are started a few rounds after the cuff is completed. The thumb gusset will wrap around the angled portion of the thumb and provide the base to which the thumb stitches are attached to form a tube (6). Markers are used to delineate the

(continued)

5

6

beginning and end of the gusset section. You'll find it easier to use the same color markers for the gusset but make sure their color contrasts to the color used for the BOR marker. I find it easiest to put all the gusset stitches on one needle (see illustration #6, page 11). Once the markers are set it's easy to get into a rhythm of knitting increase rows followed by plain knit rows. Depending on the size you are making some of the rows will be skipped, so pay attention to the specific directions for the size you are making. Also, the larger sizes require more rows, so pay attention to the direction to proceed ahead for the smaller sizes.

Round 4: Knit 14 (16, 16, 18) (18, 20, 20, 22) sts, pm, k1, pm, k to end of round.

Round 5: Knit to first marker, sm, M1L, k1, M1R, sm, k to end of round—3 sts between gusset markers.

Round 6: Knit to end of round, slipping markers as you come to them.

Round 7 for size 1 and 4 only: Knit to end of round, slipping markers as you come to them. Skip for other sizes.

Round 8: Knit to first marker, sm, M1L, knit to next marker, M1R, sm, k to end of round—5 sts between markers.

Round 9: Knit to end of round, slipping markers as you come to them.

Round 10 for size 1 and 4 only: Knit to end of round, slipping markers as you come to them. Skip for other sizes.

Round 11: Knit to first marker, sm, M1L, knit to next marker, M1R, sm, k to end of round—7 sts between markers.

Round 12: Knit to end of round, slipping markers as you come to them.

Round 13 for sizes 1, 2, 3, 4, and 6 only: Knit to end of round, slipping markers as you come to them. Skip for other sizes.

Round 14: Knit to first marker, sm, M1L, knit to next marker, M1R, sm, k to end of round—9 sts between markers.

Round 15: Knit to end of round, slipping markers as you come to them.

Size 1: Proceed to round 29.

Round 16 for sizes 2, 3, 4, 5, and 6 only: Knit to end of round, slipping markers as you come to them. Skip for other sizes.

Round 17 for sizes 2, 3, 4, 5, 6, 7, and 8 only: Knit to first marker, sm, M1L, knit to next marker, M1R, sm, k to end of round—11 sts between markers.

Round 18 for sizes 2, 3, 4, 5, 6, 7, and 8 only: Knit to end of round, slipping markers as you come to them.

Round 19 for size 2, 3, 4, 5, 6, and 8 only: Knit to end of round, slipping markers as you come to them. Skip for other sizes.

Sizes 2, 3, and 4: Proceed to round 29.

Round 20 for sizes 5, 6, 7, and 8 only: Knit to first marker, sm, M1L, knit to next marker, M1R, sm, k to end of round—13 sts between markers.

Rounds 21–22 for sizes 5, 6, 7, and 8 only: Knit to end of round, slipping markers as you come to them.

Size 5: Proceed to round 29.

Round 23 for sizes 6, 7, and 8 only: Knit to first marker, sm, M1L, knit to next marker, M1R, sm, k to end of round—15 sts between markers.

Rounds 24–25 for sizes 6, 7, and 8 only: Knit to end of round, slipping markers as you come to them.

Size 6: Proceed to round 29.

Round 26 for sizes 7 and 8 only: Knit to first marker, sm, M1L, knit to next marker, M1R, sm, k to end of round—17 sts between markers.

Rounds 27–28 for sizes 7 and 8 only: Knit to end of round, slipping markers as you come to them.

Round 29, all sizes: Transfer gusset stitches to holder as follows: Knit to marker, remove marker, place next 9 (11, 11, 11) (13, 15, 17, 17) sts on holder, remove marker, use backward thumb loop to cast on 1 (1, 2, 1,) (2, 1, 2, 1) st over gap left by gusset stitches, k to end of round.

Once all the gusset stitches have been completed, then a final round is worked to transfer the gusset stitches to a holder and one or more stitches is cast on to bridge the gap that is left once the stitches have been removed. You can use a small stitch holder for the gusset stitches but I prefer to use a short length (about 8" [20 cm]) of contrast yarn threaded on a yarn needle (7).

7

To make a backward thumb loop, see the directions on page 13.

The gusset sts will remain on their holder until the shaping is finished for the mitten tip (8).

8

Round 30: Knit.
Round 31 for size 1: K14, k2tog, k13.
Round 31 for size 2: K16, k2tog, k15.
Round 31 for size 4: K18, k2tog, k17.
Round 31 for size 6: K19, k2tog, k18.
Skip round 31 for sizes 3, 5, 7 and 8.
There should be:
28 (32, 34, 36) (38, 40, 42, 45) sts.
Round 32: Knit.

Repeat round 32 until length from cuff is approximately 3" (3½", 4", 4½") (5", 5½", 6", 6½") [7.5 (9, 10, 11.5) (12.5, 14, 15, 16.5) cm]. At this point, the total length from cast-on row should be 4½" (5½", 6¼", 7") (7½", 8¼", 8¾", 9½") [11.5 (14, 16, 18) (19, 21, 22, 24) cm].

SHAPE TIP OF MITTEN
Once the desired length has been completed it is time to work some decreases to taper the tip of the mitten. The shaping starts out slowly with plain knit rows between decrease rows at the beginning but the last few rows eliminate the plain knit rows between decrease rows so that the tip is more sharply tapered. Depending on the size you are making some of the rows will be skipped, so pay attention to the specific directions for the size you are making. Also, the larger sizes require more rows, so pay attention to the direction to proceed ahead for the smaller sizes.

Round 1 for size 1, 2, 4, and 6 only: Knit.
Round 1 for size 3: [Knit 15, k2tog] twice—32 sts remain.
Round 1 for size 5: [Knit 17, k2tog] twice—36 sts remain.
Round 1 for size 7: [Knit 19, k2tog] twice—40 sts remain.
Round 1 for size 8: Knit 22, k2tog, knit to end of round—44 sts remain.
Round 2: *Knit 5 (6, 6, 7) (7, 8, 8, 9) sts, k2tog*; repeat from * to * to end of round—24 (28, 28, 32) (32, 36, 36, 40) sts remain.
Round 3: Knit.

(continued)

Round 4: *Knit 4 (5, 5, 6) (6, 7, 7, 8) sts, k2tog*; repeat from * to * to end of round—20 (24, 24, 28) (28, 32, 32, 36) sts remain.

Round 5: Knit.

Round 6: *Knit 3 (4, 4, 5) (5, 6, 6, 7) sts, k2tog*; repeat from * to * to end of round—16 (20, 20, 24) (24, 28, 28, 32) sts remain.

Round 7: Knit.

Round 8: *Knit 2 (3, 3, 4) (4, 5, 5, 6) sts, k2tog*; repeat from * to * to end of round—12 (16, 16, 20) (20, 24, 24, 28) sts remain.

Round 9 for sizes 6, 7, and 8 only: Knit. Skip for other sizes.

Round 10: *Knit 1 (2, 2, 3) (3, 4, 4, 5) sts, k2tog*; repeat from * to * to end of round—8 (12, 12, 16) (16, 20, 20, 24) sts remain.

Size 1: Proceed to round 15.

Round 11 for sizes 2, 3, 4, 5, 6, 7, and 8 only: *Knit - (1, 1, 2) (2, 3, 3, 4) sts, k2tog*; repeat from * to * to end of round— - (8, 8, 12) (12, 16, 16, 20) sts remain.

Sizes 2 and 3: Proceed to round 15.

Round 12 for sizes 4, 5, 6, 7, and 8 only: *Knit - (-, -, 1) (1, 2, 2, 3) sts, k2tog*; repeat from * to * to end of round— - (-, -, 8) (8, 12, 12, 16) sts remain.

Sizes 4 and 5: Proceed to directions for finishing main portion of mitten.

Round 13 for sizes 6, 7, and 8 only: *Knit - (-, -, -) (-, 1, 1, 2) sts, k2tog*; repeat from * to * to end of round— - (-, -, -) (-, 8, 8, 12) sts remain.

Size 6 and 7: Proceed to directions for finishing main portion of mitten.

Round 14 for size 8 only: *K1, k2tog*; repeat from * to * to end of round—8 sts remain.

Size 8: Proceed to directions for finishing main portion of mitten.

Round 15 for sizes 1, 2, and 3 only: *K2tog*; repeat from * to * to end of round—4 sts remain.

FINISHING MAIN PORTION OF MITTEN

Cut yarn leaving an 8″ (20 cm) tail. Thread tail onto yarn needle and draw through remaining stitches on needle. Pull to tighten loop and pass yarn needle to inside of mitten and weave yarn tail through stitches to secure.

Once the decreases have been accomplished you will need to close the top. Cut the yarn leaving a tail at least 8" (20 cm) long and thread the tail on a yarn needle. Pass the yarn needle through the final stitches (working in the same order as you would if knitting) to form a draw string (9). Pull the tail tightly to close the hole at the top and then pass the needle through the hole to the inside of the mitten. Give the tail an extra tug on the inside and weave it through the stitches on the inside to secure.

9

MITTEN THUMB

Remove gusset stitches from stitch holder and distribute on three DPNs.

Now it's time to attach stitches to the top of the gusset which forms the base for the thumb. Remove the gusset stitches from the holder (or string) and distribute them on double-pointed needles. Begin transferring the stitches to the needles at the right side of the gap (when holding the mitten with the ribbing at the bottom) and put more stitches on the first and second needle than the third (10).

Attach yarn leaving an 8" (20 cm) tail, use the third needle to pick up and knit 3 (3, 3, 3) (4, 4, 4, 4) stitches over gap. Place marker to indicate beginning of round, join in the round and continue to knit as follows:

You will find it easier to pick up stitches over the gap if you rotate the mitten so the ribbing is at the top. Start the working yarn by picking up and knitting stitches over the gap as indicated (these stitches will be on your third needle) (11). Be sure to leave a tail at least 8" (20 cm) long. At the end of the first full round, two decreases will be worked to incorporate the picked-up stitches with the existing gusset stitches. Remember that the round begins on needle one or use a BOR marker, if desired.

Round 1 for sizes 1 (2, 3, 4): Knit until 4 sts remain before end of round, ssk, k1, k2tog (you will need to reposition the BOR marker to fall after the k2tog).

Round 1 for sizes (5, 6, 7, 8): Knit until 5 sts remain before end of round, ssk, k2, k2tog (you will need to reposition the BOR marker to fall after the k2tog). You should have 10 (12, 12, 12) (15, 17, 19, 19) sts.

Round 2: Knit.

(continued)

10

11

12

Repeat round 2 for 5 (7, 9, 9) (11, 12, 14, 14) more rows or until length from beginning of thumb (where stitches were picked up over gusset space) equals ¾" (1", 1¼", 1¼") (1½", 1¾", 2", 2") [2 (2.5, 3, 3) (4, 4.5, 5, 5) cm].

Once the thumb stitches are established you'll find that the knitting progresses very quickly (12).

SHAPE TIP OF THUMB
Work decreases to taper tip of thumb.

The decreases to shape the tip of the mitten thumb and the closing of the hole are completed in much the same way as the mitten tip, only in miniature.

Round 1 for sizes 1, 7, and 8: K2tog, knit to end of round.

Round 1 for size 6: K2tog, k6, k2tog, k to end of round.

Round 1 for all other sizes: Knit. There should be:
9 (12, 12, 12) (15, 15, 18, 18) sts.

Round 2: *K1 (2, 2, 2) (3, 3, 4, 4), k2tog*; repeat from * to * to end of round— 6 (9, 9, 9) (12, 12, 15, 15) sts remain.

Round 3: Knit.

Round 4 for size 1: *K1, k2tog*; repeat from * to * to end of round—4 sts remain.

Round 4 for size 2, 3, 4, 5, 6, 7, and 8 only: *K - (1, 1, 2) (2, 2, 3, 3), k2tog*; repeat from * to * to end of round— - (6, 6, 6) (9, 9, 12, 12) sts remain.

Sizes 1, 2, 3, and 4: Proceed to directions for finishing thumb.

Round 5 for sizes 5, 6, 7, and 8 only: *K – (-, -, -) (1, 1, 2, 2), k2tog*; repeat from * to * to end of round— - (-, -, -) (6, 6, 9, 9) sts remain.

Sizes 5 and 6: Proceed to directions for finishing thumb.

Round 6 for sizes 7 and 8 only: *K1, k2tog*; repeat from * to * to end of round—6 sts remain.

FINISHING THUMB
Remove marker and cut yarn leaving a tail at least 8" (20 cm) long. Thread tail onto yarn needle and draw through remaining stitches on needle. Pull to tighten loop and pass to inside of thumb and weave through stitches to secure. Using yarn tail at the base of the thumb, close any gaps that might remain and secure by weaving through stitches.

Repeat directions for second mitten. To finish mittens weave in all ends and steam lightly.

Mitten Extras

There are few ways to change the essential look of a mitten, but you can still express your creativity by how you get started with the cuff.

CHANGING THE CUFF

In the Mitten Power chapter most of the mittens begin with a k2, p2 ribbing. One easy way to get a different look is to make the ribbing section twice as long. Fold it back as a cuff or keep it long and tucked up your sleeve. You can also change the look of the cuff by using different stitches. For instance, try the two-stitch right twist mini cable pattern on page 6 for the mitten cuff in place of any k2, p2 ribbing.

Instead of ribbing, make the cuff in garter stitch or seed stitch. To make garter stitch in the round, alternate one round of knit with one round of purl. Seed stitch is made on an even number of stitches by working the first round as k1, p1 and the second round as p1, k1; repeat rounds 1 and 2 until the cuff is the desired length. For another cute idea, start the mitten with a rolled edge. After a few rows of all knit stitch, work two or three rows of ribbing to stop the roll and then change back to stockinette stitch (all knit).

annoying than a gusset that doesn't fit so add or subtract plain knit rows to the gusset shaping to make it longer or shorter. The same applies to the thumb—add a few rows for extra length or pick up and knit a few more stitches on the first thumb row for extra circumference.

MITTEN CORD

Nothing makes a pair of kid's mittens more special that a mitten cord! You can make a crochet chain or knit an I-cord (see photo below). Or keep it really simple by casting on enough stitches for the desired length, knit one row, and then bind off. To get the right length, measure from the center back to the wrist with the arm slightly bent and double the length. If desired, you can add a few extra inches for growing room and make a knot in the center of the cord.

CUSTOM FIT

Making a hat that fits is quite simple because human heads don't have a lot of variance in size or shape. The same does not hold true for our hands. There's a big difference between a child's hand and an adult's hand and there's a lot of variance in shape. Once you learn the basic mitten pattern you can explore some creative possibilities by modifying the pattern to fit exactly the way you want. For instance, if you have exceptionally long fingers then add some extra rows to the mitten before the tip is shaped. Nothing is more

Mitten Power

In this section, the basic mitten pattern is given in various gauges. Follow the Mitten Power instructions that are written for the gauge recommended on the yarn label. I encourage you to use high-quality, smooth wool until you become comfortable with making basic mittens. All of the mittens in this section have a ribbed cuff but you could certainly substitute a cuff of garter stitch instead.

MITTEN POWER 5.0: Size, Finished Dimensions, and Yardage

	To Fit Size	Finished Hand Circumference	Finished Length	Approximate Yardage
Size 1	2 to 4 year	5½" (14 cm)	5¾" (15 cm)	60 yd (55 m)
Size 2	5 to 7 year	6¼" (16 cm)	7" (18 cm)	80 yd (73 m)
Size 3	8 to 10 year	6¾" (17 cm)	7¾" (20 cm)	100 yd (91 m)
Size 4	12 year to Women's Small	7¼" (18 cm)	8½" (22 cm)	110 yd (101 m)
Size 5	Women's Medium	7½" (19 cm)	9" (23 cm)	130 yd (119 m)
Size 6	Women's Large/ Men's Small	8" (20 cm)	9¾" (25 cm)	150 yd (137 m)
Size 7	Men's Medium	8½" (22 cm)	10½" (27 cm)	175 yd (160 m)
Size 8	Men's Large	9" (23 cm)	11½" (29 cm)	195 yd (173 m)

Directions will be shown in the pattern as follows: Size 1 (Size 2, Size 3, Size 4) (Size 5, Size 6, Size 7, Size 8)

MITTEN POWER 5.0
5 STITCHES = 1 INCH (2.5 CM)

**CAST ON STITCHES
AND BEGIN KNITTING CUFF**
Make both mittens alike.

Using smaller needles, cast on 28 (32, 32, 36) (36, 40, 40, 44) sts. Place BOR marker and join in the round being careful not to twist (see page 20).
Round 1: *K2, p2*; repeat from * to * to end of round.

Repeat round 1 until cuff measures 1½" (2", 2¼", 2½") (2½", 2¾", 2¾", 3") [4 (5, 6, 6.5) (6.5, 7, 7, 7.5) cm].

THUMB GUSSET
Change to larger needles.
Round 1: Knit.
Round 2 for sizes 1, 2, 3, and 4: Inc 1, knit to end of round.
Round 2 for sizes 5, 6, 7, and 8: Knit.
Round 3 for sizes 5, 6, 7, and 8 only: Inc 1, knit to end of round. Skip for other sizes.
There should be:
29, (33, 33, 37) (37, 41, 41, 45) sts.
Round 4: Knit 14 (16, 16, 18) (18, 20, 20, 22) sts, pm, k1, pm, k to end of round.

GAUGE

20 sts = 4" (10 cm) in stockinette stitch

YARN

Medium weight yarn; the approximate yardage for each size is shown in the chart at left.

NEEDLES AND NOTIONS

US size 7 (4.5 mm) double-pointed needles or size required to achieve gauge

US size 5 (3.75 mm) double-pointed needles (or two sizes smaller than size used to achieve gauge)

Circular stitch markers

Yarn needle for weaving in ends

Round 5: Knit to first marker, sm, M1L, k1, M1R, sm, k to end of round—3 sts between gusset markers.

Round 6: Knit to end of round, slipping markers as you come to them.

Round 7 for size 1 and 4 only: Knit to end of round, slipping markers as you come to them. Skip for other sizes.

Round 8: Knit to first marker, sm, M1L, knit to next marker, M1R, sm, k to end of round—5 sts between markers.

Round 9: Repeat round 6.

Round 10 for size 1 and 4 only: Repeat round 6. Skip for other sizes.

Round 11: Knit to first marker, sm, M1L, knit to next marker, M1R, sm, k to end of round—7 sts between markers.

Round 12: Repeat round 6.

Round 13 for sizes 1, 2, 3, 4, and 6 only: Repeat round 6. Skip for other sizes.

Round 14: Knit to first marker, sm, M1L, knit to next marker, M1R, sm, k to end of round—9 sts between markers.

Round 15: Repeat round 6.

Size 1: Proceed to round 29.

Round 16 for sizes 2, 3, 4, 5, and 6 only: Repeat round 6. Skip for other sizes.

Round 17 for sizes 2, 3, 4, 5, 6, 7, and 8 only: Knit to first marker, sm, M1L, knit to next marker, M1R, sm, k to end of round—11 sts between markers.

Round 18 for sizes 2, 3, 4, 5, 6, 7, and 8 only: Repeat round 6.

Round 19 for size 2, 3, 4, 5, 6, and 8 only: Repeat round 6. Skip for other sizes.

Sizes 2, 3, and 4: Proceed to round 29.

Round 20 for sizes 5, 6, 7, and 8 only: Knit to first marker, sm, M1L, knit to next marker, M1R, sm, k to end of round—13 sts between markers.

Rounds 21–22 for sizes 5, 6, 7, and 8 only: Repeat round 6.

Size 5: Proceed to round 29.

Round 23 for sizes 6, 7, and 8 only: Knit to first marker, sm, M1L, knit to next marker, M1R, sm, k to end of round—15 sts between markers.

Rounds 24–25 for sizes 6, 7, and 8 only: Repeat round 6.

Size 6: Proceed to round 29.

Round 26 for sizes 7 and 8 only: Knit to first marker, sm, M1L, knit to next marker, M1R, sm, k to end of round—17 sts between markers.

Rounds 27–28 for sizes 7 and 8 only: Repeat round 6.

Round 29, all sizes: Knit to marker, remove marker, place next 9 (11, 11, 11) (13, 15, 17, 17) sts on holder, remove marker, use backward thumb loop to cast on 1 (1, 2, 1,) (2, 1, 2, 1) st over gap left by gusset stitches, k to end of round.

Round 30: Knit.

Round 31 for size 1: K14, k2tog, k13.

Round 31 for size 2: K16, k2tog, k15.

Round 31 for size 4: K18, k2tog, k17.

Round 31 for size 6: K19, k2tog, k18.

Skip round 31 for sizes 3, 5, 7 and 8.

There should be:
28 (32, 34, 36) (38, 40, 42, 45) sts.

(continued)

Round 32: Knit.

Repeat round 32 until length from cuff is approximately 3" (3½", 4", 4½") (5", 5½", 6", 6½") [7.5 (9, 10, 11.5) (12.5, 14, 15, 16.5) cm]. At this point, the total length from cast-on row should be 4½" (5½", 6¼", 7") (7½", 8¼", 8¾", 9½") [11.5 (14, 16, 18) (19, 21, 22, 24) cm].

SHAPE TIP OF MITTEN

Work decreases to shape the tip of the mitten.

Round 1 for size 1, 2, 4, and 6 only: Knit.

Round 1 for size 3: [Knit 15, k2tog] twice—32 sts remain.

Round 1 for size 5: [Knit 17, k2tog] twice—36 sts remain.

Round 1 for size 7: [Knit 19, k2tog] twice—40 sts remain.

Round 1 for size 8: Knit 22, k2tog, knit to end of round—44 sts remain.

Round 2: *Knit 5 (6, 6, 7) (7, 8, 8, 9) sts, k2tog*; repeat from * to * to end of round—24 (28, 28, 32) (32, 36, 36, 40) sts remain.

Round 3: Knit.

Round 4: *Knit 4 (5, 5, 6) (6, 7, 7, 8) sts, k2tog*; repeat from * to * to end of round—20 (24, 24, 28) (28, 32, 32, 36) sts remain.

Round 5: Knit.

Round 6: *Knit 3 (4, 4, 5) (5, 6, 6, 7) sts, k2tog*; repeat from * to * to end of round—16 (20, 20, 24) (24, 28, 28, 32) sts remain.

Round 7: Knit.

Round 8: *Knit 2 (3, 3, 4) (4, 5, 5, 6) sts, k2tog*; repeat from * to * to end of round—12 (16, 16, 20) (20, 24, 24, 28) sts remain.

Round 9 for sizes 6, 7, and 8 only: Knit. Skip for other sizes.

Round 10: *Knit 1 (2, 2, 3) (3, 4, 4, 5) sts, k2tog*; repeat from * to * to end of round—8 (12, 12, 16) (16, 20, 20, 24) sts remain.

Size 1: Proceed to round 15.

Round 11 for sizes 2, 3, 4, 5, 6, 7, and 8 only: *Knit - (1, 1, 2) (2, 3, 3, 4) sts, k2tog*; repeat from * to * to end of round— - (8, 8, 12) (12, 16, 16, 20) sts remain.

Sizes 2 and 3: Proceed to round 15.

Round 12 for sizes 4, 5, 6, 7, and 8 only: *Knit - (-, -, 1) (1, 2, 2, 3) sts, k2tog*; repeat from * to * to end of round— - (-, -, 8) (8, 12, 12, 16) sts remain.

Sizes 4 and 5: Proceed to directions for finishing main portion of mitten.

Round 13 for sizes 6, 7, and 8 only: *Knit - (-, -, -) (-, 1, 1, 2) sts, k2tog*; repeat from * to * to end of round— - (-, -, -) (-, 8, 8, 12) sts remain.

Size 6 and 7: Proceed to directions for finishing main portion of mitten.

Round 14 for size 8 only: *K1, k2tog*; repeat from * to * to end of round— 8 sts remain.

Size 8: Proceed to directions for finishing main portion of mitten.

Round 15 for sizes 1, 2, and 3 only: *K2tog*; repeat from * to * to end of round—4 sts remain.

FINISHING MAIN PORTION OF MITTEN

Cut yarn leaving an 8" (20 cm) tail. Thread tail onto yarn needle and draw through remaining stitches on needle. Pull to tighten loop and pass yarn needle to inside of mitten and weave yarn tail through stitches to secure.

MITTEN THUMB

Remove gusset stitches from stitch holder and distribute on three DPNs. Attach yarn leaving an 8" (20 cm) tail, pick up and knit 3 (3, 3, 3) (4, 4, 4, 4) stitches over gap. Place marker to indicate beginning of round, join in the round and continue to knit as follows:

Round 1 for sizes 1 (2, 3, 4): Knit until 4 sts remain before end of round, ssk, k1, k2tog (you will need to reposition the BOR marker to fall after the k2tog).

Round 1 for sizes (5, 6, 7, 8): Knit until 5 sts remain before end of round, ssk, k2, k2tog (you will need to reposition the BOR marker to fall after the k2tog).
You should have:
10 (12, 12, 12) (15, 17, 19, 19) sts.
Round 2: Knit.

Repeat round 2 for 5 (7, 9, 9) (11, 12, 14, 14) more rows or until length from beginning of thumb (where stitches were picked up over gusset space) equals ¾" (1", 1¼", 1¼") (1½", 1¾", 2", 2") [2 (2.5, 3, 3) (4, 4.5, 5, 5) cm].

SHAPE TIP OF THUMB
Work decreases to taper tip of thumb.
Round 1 for sizes 1, 7, and 8: K2tog, knit to end of round.
Round 1 for size 6: K2tog, k6, k2tog, k to end of round.
Round 1 for all other sizes: Knit.
There should be:
9 (12, 12, 12) (15, 15, 18, 18) sts.
Round 2: *K1 (2, 2, 2) (3, 3, 4, 4), k2tog*; repeat from * to * to end of round— 6 (9, 9, 9) (12, 12, 15, 15) sts remain.
Round 3: Knit.
Round 4 for size 1: *K1, k2tog*; repeat from * to * to end of round—4 sts remain.

Round 4 for size 2, 3, 4, 5, 6, 7, and 8 only: *K - (1, 1, 2) (2, 2, 3, 3), k2tog*; repeat from * to * to end of round— - (6, 6, 6) (9, 9, 12, 12) sts remain.
Sizes 1, 2, 3, and 4: Proceed to directions for finishing thumb.
Round 5 for sizes 5, 6, 7, and 8 only: *K – (-, -, -) (1, 1, 2, 2), k2tog*; repeat from * to * to end of round— - (-, -, -) (6, 6, 9, 9) sts remain.
Sizes 5 and 6: Proceed to directions for finishing thumb.
Round 6 for sizes 7 and 8 only: *K1, k2tog*; repeat from * to * to end of round—6 sts remain.

FINISHING THUMB
Cut yarn leaving a tail at least 8" (20 cm) long. Thread tail onto yarn needle and draw through remaining stitches on needle. Pull to tighten loop and pass to inside of thumb and weave through stitches to secure. Using yarn tail at the base of the thumb, close any gaps that might remain and secure by weaving through stitches.

Repeat directions for second mitten. To finish mittens weave in all ends and steam lightly.

MITTEN POWER 3.5: Size, Finished Dimensions, and Yardage

	To Fit Size	Finished Hand Circumference	Finished Length	Approximate Yardage
Size 1	7 to 10 year	6½" (17 cm)	7¾" (20 cm)	75 yd (69 m)
Size 2	12 year to Women's Small	7" (18 cm)	8½" (22 cm)	85 yd (78 m)
Size 3	Women's Med.	7½" (19 cm)	9" (23 cm)	95 yd (87 m)
Size 4	Women's Large/ Men's Small	8" (20 cm)	9½" (24 cm)	115 yd (105 m)
Size 5	Men's Medium	8½" (22 cm)	10½" (27 cm)	130 yd (119 m)
Size 6	Men's Large	9" (23 cm)	11½" (29 cm)	145 yd (133 m)

Directions will be shown in the pattern as follows: Size 1 (Size 2, Size 3) (Size 4, Size 5, Size 6)

MITTEN POWER 3.5
3½ STITCHES = 1 INCH (2.5 CM)

CAST ON STITCHES AND BEGIN KNITTING CUFF
Make both mittens alike.

Using smaller needles, cast on 20 (24, 24) (28, 28, 32) sts. Place BOR marker and join in the round being careful not to twist (see page 20).

Round 1: *K2, p2*; repeat from * to * to end of round.

Repeat round 1 until cuff measures 2" (2¼", 2½") (2¾", 2¾", 3") [5 (6, 6.5) (7, 7, 7.5) cm].

THUMB GUSSET
Change to larger needles.

Round 1: Knit.

Round 2 for sizes 1 and 2 only: Inc 1, knit to end of round.

Round 2 for all other sizes: Knit.

Round 3 for sizes 3, 4, 5, and 6 only: Inc 1, knit to end of round. Skip for other sizes.

There should be:
21 (25, 25) (29, 29, 33) sts.

Round 4: Knit 10 (12, 12) (14, 14, 16) sts, pm, k1, pm, k to end of round.

Round 5: Knit to first marker, sm, M1L, k1, M1R, sm, k to end of round—3 sts between gusset markers.

Round 6: Knit to end of round, slipping markers as you come to them.

Round 7: Knit to first marker, sm, M1L, knit to next marker, M1R, sm, k to end of round—5 sts between markers.

Round 8: Repeat round 6.

Round 9 for sizes 2, 3, 4, and 5 only: Repeat round 6. Skip for other sizes.

Round 10: Knit to first marker, sm, M1L, knit to next marker, M1R, sm, k to end of round—7 sts between markers.

Round 11: Repeat round 6.

Round 12 for sizes 1, 2, 3, 4, and 5 only: Repeat round 6. Skip for other sizes.

Round 13: Knit to first marker, sm, M1L, knit to next marker, M1R, sm, k to end of round—9 sts between markers.

Round 14: Repeat round 6.

Size 1, 2, and 3: Proceed to round 21.

Round 15 for sizes 4, 5, and 6 only: Repeat round 6.

Round 16 for sizes 4, 5, and 6 only: Knit to first marker, sm, M1L, knit to next marker, M1R, sm, k to end of round—11 sts between markers.

GAUGE

14 sts and 20 rows = 4" (10 cm) in stockinette stitch

YARN

Bulky weight yarn; the approximate yardage for each size is shown in the chart at left.

NEEDLES AND NOTIONS

US size 10½ (6.5 mm) double-pointed needles or size required to achieve gauge

US size 9 (5.5 mm) double-pointed needles (or two sizes smaller than size used to achieve gauge)

Circular stitch markers

Small stitch holder (or waste yarn)

Yarn needle for weaving in ends

Rounds 17 for sizes 4, 5, and 6 only: Repeat round 6 twice.

Sizes 4 and 5: Proceed to round 21.

Round 18 for size 6 only: Repeat round 6.

Round 19 for size 6 only: Knit to first marker, sm, M1L, knit to next marker, M1R, sm, k to end of round—13 sts between markers.

Round 20 for size 6 only: Repeat round 6.

Round 21: Knit to marker, remove marker, place next 9 (9, 9) (11, 11, 13) sts on holder, remove marker, use backward thumb loop to cast on 2 (1, 2) (1, 2, 1) sts over gap left by gusset stitches, k to end of round.

Round 22: Knit.

Round 23 for size 2: K12, k2tog, knit to end of round.

Round 23 for size 4: K14, k2tog, knit to end of round.

Round 23 for size 6: K16, k2tog, knit to end of round. Skip round 23 for sizes 1, 3 and 5.

There should be:

22 (24, 26) (28, 30, 32) sts.

Round 24: Knit.

Repeat round 24 until length from cuff is approximately 4¼" (4¾", 5") (5¾", 6", 6½") [11 (12, 12.5) (14.5, 15, 16.5) cm]. At this point, the total length from cast-on row should be 6¼" (7", 7½") (8", 8¾", 9½") [16 (18, 19) (20, 22, 24) cm].

SHAPE TIP OF MITTEN

Work decreases to shape the tip of the mitten.

Round 1 for sizes 2, 4, and 6 only: Knit.

Round 1 for size 1: [Knit 9, k2tog] twice—20 sts remain.

Round 1 for size 3: [Knit 11, k2tog] twice—24 sts remain.

Round 1 for size 5: [Knit 13, k2tog] twice—28 sts remain.

Round 2: *Knit 3 (4, 4) (5, 5, 6) sts, k2tog*; repeat from * to * to end of round—16 (20, 20) (24, 24, 28) sts remain.

Round 3: Knit.

Round 4: *Knit 2 (3, 3) (4, 4, 5) sts, k2tog*; repeat from * to * to end of round—12 (16, 16) (20, 20, 24) sts remain.

Round 5: Knit.

Round 6: *Knit 1 (2, 2) (3, 3, 4) sts, k2tog*; repeat from * to * to end of round—8 (12, 12) (16, 16, 20) sts remain.

Size 1: Proceed to round 11.

Round 7 for size 6 only: Knit. Skip for other sizes.

Round 8 for sizes 2, 3, 4, 5, and 6 only: *Knit - (1, 1) (2, 2, 3) sts, k2tog*; repeat from * to * to end of round— - (8, 8) (12, 12, 16) sts remain.

Size 2 and 3: Proceed to round 11.

Round 9 for sizes 4, 5, and 6 only: *Knit - (-, -) (1, 1, 2) sts, k2tog*; repeat from * to * to end of round— - (-, -) (8, 8, 12) sts remain.

(continued)

Size 4 and 5: Proceed to round 11.
Round 10 for size 6 only: *K1, k2tog*; repeat from * to * to end of round—8 sts remain.
Round 11: *K2tog*; repeat from * to * to end of round—4 sts remain.

FINISHING MAIN PORTION OF MITTEN

Cut yarn leaving an 8" (20 cm) tail. Thread tail onto yarn needle and draw through remaining stitches on needle. Pull to tighten loop and pass yarn needle to inside of mitten and weave yarn tail through stitches to secure.

MITTEN THUMB

Remove gusset stitches from stitch holder and distribute on three DPNs. Attach yarn leaving an 8" (20 cm) tail, pick up and knit 3 (3, 3) (4, 4, 4) stitches over gap. Place marker to indicate beginning of round, join in the round and continue to knit as follows:

Round 1 for sizes 1, 2, and 3: Knit until 4 sts remain before end of round, ssk, k1, k2tog (you will need to reposition the BOR marker to fall after the k2tog).

Round 1 for sizes 5, 6, 7, and 8: Knit until 5 sts remain before end of round, ssk, k2, k2tog (you will need to reposition the BOR marker to fall after the k2tog).

There should be:
10 (10, 10) (13, 13, 15) sts.

Round 2: Knit.

Repeat round 2 for 6 (6, 8) (9, 10, 10) more rows or until length from beginning of thumb (where stitches were picked up over gusset space) equals 1¼" (1¼", 1½") (1¾", 2", 2") [3 (3 4) (4.5, 5, 5) cm].

SHAPE TIP OF THUMB

Work decreases to taper tip of thumb.
Round 1 for sizes 1, 2, 3, 4, and 5: K2tog, knit to end of round.
Round 1 for size 6: Knit.
There should be: 9 (9, 9) (12, 12, 15) sts.
Round 2: *K1 (1, 1) (2, 2, 3), k2tog*; repeat from * to * to end of round–6 (6, 6) (9, 9, 12) sts remain.
Round 3: Knit.
Size 1, 2 and 3: Proceed to round 7.
Round 5 for sizes 4, 5, and 6 only: *Knit - (-, -) (1, 1, 2) sts, k2tog*; repeat from * to * to end of round— - (-, -) (6, 6, 9) sts remain.
Size 4 and 5: Proceed to round 7.
Round 6 for size 6 only: *K1, k2tog*; repeat from * to * to end of round—6 sts remain.
Round 7: *K1, k2tog*—4 sts remain.

FINISHING THUMB

Cut yarn leaving a tail at least 8" (20 cm) long. Thread tail onto yarn needle and draw through remaining stitches on needle. Pull to tighten loop and pass to inside of thumb and weave through stitches to secure. Using yarn tail at the base of the thumb, close any gaps that might remain and secure by weaving through stitches.

Repeat directions for second mitten. To finish mittens weave in all ends and steam lightly.

MITTEN POWER 2.5: Size, Finished Dimensions, and Yardage

	To Fit Size	Finished Hand Circumference	Finished Length	Approximate Yardage
Size 1	12 year to Women's Small	7" (18 cm)	8½" (22 cm)	60 yd (55 m)
Size 2	Women's Med.	7½" (19 cm)	9" (23 cm)	70 yd (64 m)
Size 3	Women's Large/Men's Small	8" (20 cm)	9½" (24 cm)	80 yd (73 m)
Size 4	Men's Medium	8½" (22 cm)	10½" (27 cm)	90 yd (82 m)
Size 5	Men's Large	9" (23 cm)	11½" (29 cm)	100 yd (91 m)

Directions will be shown in the pattern as follows: Size 1 (Size 2, Size 3, Size 4, Size 5)

MITTEN POWER 2.5
2½ STITCHES = 1 INCH (2.5 CM)

CAST ON STITCHES AND BEGIN KNITTING CUFF
Make both mittens alike.

Using smaller needles, cast on 18 (18, 20, 20, 22) sts. Place BOR marker and join in the round being careful not to twist (see page 20).

Round 1: *K1, p1*; repeat from * to * to end of round.

Repeat round 1 until cuff measures 1¼" (1¼", 1½", 1½", 1¾") [3 (3, 4, 4, 4.5) cm].

THUMB GUSSET
Change to larger needles.

Rounds 1–3: Knit.

Round 4 for size 1: Inc 1, knit to end of round.

Round 4 for sizes 2, 3, 4, and 5: Knit.

Round 5 for sizes 2, 3, 4, and 5: Inc 1, knit to end of round. Skip for other sizes.

(continued)

GAUGE
10 sts and 16 rows = 4" (10 cm) in stockinette stitch

YARN
Super bulky weight yarn; the approximate yardage for each size is shown in the chart above.

NEEDLES AND NOTIONS
US size 15 (10 mm) double-pointed needles or size required to achieve gauge

US size 11 (8 mm) double-pointed needles (or two sizes smaller than size used to achieve gauge)

Optional Magic Loop: above needle sizes in a circular needle at least 32" (81 cm) long.

Circular stitch markers

Yarn needle for weaving in ends

There should be: 19 (19, 21, 21, 23) sts.

Round 6: Knit 9 (9, 10, 10, 11) sts, pm, k1, pm, k to end of round.

Round 7: Knit to first marker, sm, M1L, k1, M1R, sm, k to end of round—3 sts between gusset markers.

Round 8: Knit to end of round, slipping markers as you come to them.

Round 9 for size 2 only: Repeat round 8. Skip for other sizes.

Round 10: Knit to first marker, sm, M1L, knit to next marker, M1R, sm, k to end of round—5 sts between markers.

Round 11: Repeat round 8.

Round 12 for sizes 1, 2, and 5 only: Repeat round 8. Skip for other sizes.

Round 13: Knit to first marker, sm, M1L, knit to next marker, M1R, sm, k to end of round—7 sts between markers.

Round 14: Repeat round 8.

Sizes 1 and 2: Proceed to round 18.

Round 15 for sizes 4, and 5 only: Repeat round 8. Skip for other sizes.

Round 16 for sizes 3, 4, and 5 only: Knit to first marker, sm, M1L, knit to next marker, M1R, sm, k to end of round—9 sts between markers.

Round 17 for sizes 3, 4, and 5 only: Repeat round 8.

Round 18: Knit to marker, remove marker, place next 7 (7, 9, 9, 9) sts on holder, remove marker, use backward thumb loop to cast on 1 st over gap left by gusset stitches, k to end of round.

Round 19: Knit.

Round 20 for size 1 only: K9, k2tog, knit to end of round.

Round 20 for size 3 only: K10, k2tog, knit to end of round. Skip round 20 for sizes 2, 4 and 5.

There should be: 18 (19, 20, 21, 23) sts.

Round 21: Knit.

Repeat round 21 until length from cuff is approximately 5¾" (6¼", 6¾", 7¼", 7¾") [14.5 (16, 17, 18.5, 19.5) cm]. At this point, the total length from cast-on row should be 7" (7½", 8¼", 8¾", 9½") [18 (19, 21, 22, 24) cm].

SHAPE TIP OF MITTEN

Work decreases to shape the tip of the mitten.

Round 1 for size 1: [Knit 7, k2tog] twice—16 sts remain.

Round 1 for size 2: [K3, k2tog] 3 times, k4—16 sts remain.

Round 1 for size 3: Knit.

Round 1 for size 4: K10, k2tog, knit to end of round, 20 sts remain.

Round 1 for size 5: [K4, k2tog] 3 times, k5, 20 sts remain.

Round 2: *Knit 2 (2, 3, 3, 3) sts, k2tog*; repeat from * to * to end of round—12 (12, 16, 16, 16) sts remain.

Round 3: Knit.

Round 4: *Knit 1 (1, 2, 2, 2) sts, k2tog*; repeat from * to * to end of round—8 (8, 12, 12, 12) sts remain.

Sizes 1 and 2: Proceed to round 7.

Round 5 for size 3, 4, and 5 only: Knit.

Round 6 for size 3, 4, and 5 only: *K1, k2tog*; repeat from * to * to end of round—8 sts remain.

Round 7: *K2tog*; repeat from * to * to end of round—4 sts remain.

FINISHING MAIN PORTION OF MITTEN

Cut yarn leaving an 8" (20 cm) tail. Thread tail onto yarn needle and draw through remaining stitches on needle. Pull to tighten loop and pass yarn needle to inside of mitten and weave yarn tail through stitches to secure.

MITTEN THUMB

Remove gusset stitches from stitch holder and distribute on three DPNs.

Attach yarn leaving an 8" (20 cm)tail, pick up and knit 3 stitches over gap. Place marker to indicate beginning of round, join in the round and continue to knit as follows:

Round 1: Knit until 4 sts remain before end of round, ssk, k1, k2tog (you will need to reposition the BOR marker to fall after the k2tog).
There should be: 8 (8, 10, 10, 10) sts.
Round 2: Knit.

Repeat Round 2 for 5 (6, 7, 8, 8) more rows or until length from beginning of thumb (where stitches were picked up over gusset space) equals 1¼" (1½", 1¾", 2", 2") [3 (4, 4.5, 5, 5) cm].

SHAPE TIP OF THUMB

Work decreases to taper tip of thumb.
Round 1 for sizes 3, 4, and 5: K2tog, knit to end of round. Skip round 1 for other sizes.
There should be: 8 (8, 9, 9, 9) sts.

Round 2 for sizes 1 and 2:
K2tog; repeat from * to * to end of round—4 sts remain.
Round 2 for sizes 3, 4, and 5:
K1, k2tog; repeat from * to * to end of round—6 sts remain.
Round 3: Knit.
Sizes 1 and 2: Proceed to directions for finishing thumb.
Round 4 for sizes 3, 4, and 5 only:
K2tog; repeat from * to * to end of round—3 sts remain.

FINISHING THUMB

Cut yarn leaving a tail at least 8" (20 cm) long. Thread tail onto yarn needle and draw through remaining stitches on needle. Pull to tighten loop and pass to inside of thumb and weave through stitches to secure. Using yarn tail at the base of the thumb, close any gaps that might remain and secure by weaving through stitches.

Repeat directions for second mitten. To finish mittens weave in all ends and steam lightly.

Mitten Gallery

Now that you've learned the basics of making mittens you'll be able to experiment with different yarns. Make the same pattern in different sizes and colors. Get inspired by trying different yarn weights and fiber compositions. All of these examples follow the simple patterns in the Mitten Power section.

ANY COLOR/ANY SIZE

In just about any yarn shop you will find that worsted weight yarn is available in the greatest variety. In one brand alone, a shop may carry over one hundred different colors. It's fun to experiment with some of the subtle variations such as solid, heather, and tweed.

Pattern: 5 sts = 1" (2.5 cm)

Size: The large size pair, shown in blue/green tweed, is size 5, women's medium. The medium size pair, shown in gold heather, is size 3, 8 to 10 years. The small size pair, shown in solid aqua, is size 1, 2 to 4 years.

Large size pair yarn: Medium weight smooth yarn, 150 yd (137 m)

Medium size pair yarn: Medium weight smooth yarn, 100 yd (91 m)

Small size pair yarn: Medium weight smooth yarn, 60 yd (55 m)

WARM AND COZY

Nothing feels better on a winter day than mittens made of thick yarn making your hands feel warm and cozy. This yarn has just enough mohair to add some fuzzy comfort to the warmth of merino.

Pattern: 3.5 sts = 1" (2.5 cm)

Size: The size shown is size 3, women's medium

Yarn: Bulky weight smooth yarn, 95 yd (87 m)

INSTANT SUCCESS

If you've already made the hat out of super bulky yarn, then you know that just a movie or two is all that's required to make these mittens (okay, maybe an epic). With this heavy yarn, a simple k1, p1 ribbing for a few rows is all that's needed for a cuff. Hand-dyed yarns are simply charming, but the colors can be quirky and these mittens are the perfect example. Believe it or not, those are the same color! Instead of being dismayed by the color difference between the two balls, I decided to make the best of it and create some interest with a few stripes.

Pattern: 2.5 sts = 1" (2.5 cm)

Variations: A contrast shade was used for the ribbing and to put a stripe in the mittens and thumb.

Size: The size shown is size 2, women's medium

Yarn: Super bulky weight single ply yarn, 70 yd (64 m) total: 45 yd (41 m) green, 25 yd (23 m) pink)

Abbreviations

Here is the list of standard abbreviations used for knitting. Until you can readily identify them, keep the list handy whenever you knit.

2-st RT	two-stitch right twist		p3tog	purl three together
4-st RKC	four-stitch right knit cross		pf&b	purl front and back
6-st RKC	six-stitch right knit cross		pm	place marker
BOR	beginning of round		psso	pass slipped stitch over
cm	centimeter		rm	remove marker
dpn(s)	double pointed needles		rs	right side
g	gram		ws	wrong side
inc	increase (lifted increase)		sl	slip
K, k	knit		sm	slip marker
k2tog	knit two together		ssk	slip, slip, knit
k3tog	knit three together		SSP	Slip Stitch Pattern
kf&b	knit front and back		st	stitch
LYS	local yarn shop		sts	stitches
m	meter		wyib	with yarn in back
M1L	make one left		wyif	with yarn in front
M1LP	make one left - purl		yo	yarnover
M1R	make one right		* *	repeat instructions
M1RP	make one right - purl			between * as directed
P, p	purl		[ ]	repeat instructions enclosed
p2tog	purl two together			by brackets as directed

CPSIA information can be obtained
at www.ICGtesting.com
Printed in the USA
LVOW06s0326250217
525377LV00002B/3/P